LEADING WOMEN

Media Mogul and Philanthropist

Oprah Winfrey

TATIANA RYCKMAN

Cavendish
Square

New York

Library of Congress Cataloging-in-Publication Data

Names: Ryckman, Tatiana, author.
Title: Oprah Winfrey : media mogul and philanthropist / Tatiana Ryckman.
Description: New York : Cavendish Square Publishing, [2017] | Series: Leading
women | Includes bibliographical references and index. | Description based
on print version record and CIP data provided by publisher; resource not
viewed.
Identifiers: LCCN 2015050660 (print) | LCCN 2015050254 (ebook) | ISBN
9781502619846 (ebook) | ISBN 9781502619839 (library bound)
Subjects: LCSH: Winfrey, Oprah. | Television personalities--United
States--Biography. | Actors--United States--Biography.
Classification: LCC PN1992.4.W56 (print) | LCC PN1992.4.W56 R93 2017 (ebook)
DDC LC record available at http://lccn.loc.gov/2015050660

Editorial Director: David McNamara
Editor: Elizabeth Schmermund
Copy Editor: Rebecca Rohan
Art Director: Jeffrey Talbot
Designer: Stephanie Flecha
Senior Production Manager: Jennifer Ryder-Talbot
Production Editor: Renni Johnson
Photo Research: J8 Media

The photographs in this book are used by permission and through the courtesy of: Everett
Collection/Shutterstock.com, cover; Barry King/Getty Images, 1; Supplied by PacificCoastNews/
Newscom, 4, 11; Nashville Public Library, Special Collections, 8; Seth Poppel Yearbook Library, 15;
Afro American Newspapers/Gado/Getty Images, 16, 28, 38; Film Favorites/Getty Images, 18; AP
Photo/Jason Lee, 22; AP Photo/Lennox McLendon, 25; Fairfax Media/Fairfax Media via Getty
Images, 30; AP Photo/Charlie Knoblock, 33; Julie Alissi/J8 Media, 34; STR/REUTERS/Newscom,
42; Ron Galella, Ltd./WireImage, 45; Heather Wines/CBS via Getty Images, 50; STEPHANE
DE SAKUTIN/AFP/Getty Images, 52; AP Photo/Charlie Bennet, 57; ZUMA Press Inc/Alamy
Stock Photo, 62; Per-Anders Pettersson/Getty Images, 64; Michelly Rall/WireImage, 69; Jocelyn
Augustino/FEMA/File:FEMA - 15020 - Photograph by Jocelyn Augustino taken on 08-30-2005 in
Louisiana.jpg/Wikimedia Commons, 73; Darren McCollester/Getty Images, 76; Frederick M. Brown/
Getty Images for NAACP Image Awards 80; Mark Von Holden/AP for Oprah Winfrey Network, 91;
Photos 12/Alamy Stock Photo, 93.

CONTENTS

CHAPTER ONE

A Humble Beginning

O prah Winfrey, a media titan and one of the most influential women in the world, wasn't born wealthy. In fact, she wasn't even born with the name Oprah. On January 29, 1954, Orpah Gail Winfrey was born to a poor, single, teen mother in Kosciusko, Mississippi. Her mother, Vernita Lee, named Orpah for a Biblical character in the book of Ruth. The name Orpah alludes to great things coming under the cover of darkness. There was no way to know at that time just how fitting the name was for the future star. It wasn't until later, when her name had been

Even at a young age, Winfrey showed promise as a performer, winning many awards, such as the Miss Fire Prevention contest in Nashville, Tennessee.

mispronounced as "Oprah" for years, that she took on the new name and built a multibillion-dollar empire around it.

On The Move

When she was born, Winfrey's family was very poor. They lived without electricity or running water. Despite her financial struggles, her grandmother, Hattie Mae Lee, cared for her granddaughter. Oprah's mother moved north to Milwaukee, Wisconsin, to find work when Oprah was only a few years old. Hattie Mae was strict but encouraging, and she taught Oprah to read at an early age. Even today, Winfrey considers learning to read as fundamental to her success as an adult. She says, "Books were my pass to personal freedom. I learned to read at age three and discovered there was a whole world to conquer that went beyond our farm in Mississippi."

By age three, Winfrey was reciting scripture in front of her church congregation. As further proof of her quick mind and talent, she entered kindergarten in 1959 but was quickly accelerated to first grade.

North to Milwaukee

Oprah liked living in Mississippi with her grandmother, so she was devastated when her grandmother became ill and was no longer able to care for her. Only six years old, she was sent north to Milwaukee to live with her mother. Vernita Lee had found work cleaning houses and had given birth to Oprah's half-sister, Patricia. Meanwhile, her father, Vernon Winfrey, had moved to Nashville, Tennessee. Even worse, on her first night in Milwaukee, she was not allowed to sleep inside the house:

> *I suddenly land in a place that is completely foreign to me. I don't know anybody, I don't really even know my mother … I walked into that space feeling completely alone and abandoned without any understanding of why I was being sent away. I was put outside to sleep … I later realized it was because of the color of my skin. My mother was boarding with this very light-skinned black woman, who could have passed for white, and I could tell instantly when I walked in the room she didn't like me.*

A Young Talent in Nashville

Feeling unwelcome was not Winfrey's only obstacle in this new home. Unable to work the long hours demanded of her while also caring for her children, Vernita sent Winfrey off again, this time to Nashville to live with Vernon and his wife, Zelma. Vernon had given up his work as a coal miner and worked as a janitor at two different schools. Though he, too, worked long days, Vernon and Zelma paid attention to Oprah and encouraged her in her studies. They had purchased a two-story brick house and were excited to have her join them, as they were unable to have children of their own.

For the first time in her young life, Winfrey had a room of her own. She enjoyed being with her father and

The Nashville Library was one of Winfrey's favorite places growing up because books made it possible to go anywhere.

stepmother. Once again Winfrey's advanced reading skills and sharp intelligence led her to skip a grade at her new school, Wharton Elementary. Worried she would be unprepared for her advanced grade, Winfrey's parents spent many hours throughout the summer of 1962 tutoring her in math and language arts so she would be ready for third grade in the fall.

When she finally started at her new school, Winfrey excelled. At that time, public schools set aside time for Bible studies and devotion, and Winfrey was frequently asked by her favorite teacher, Mrs. Duncan, to lead these devotions. Mrs. Duncan was influential in helping her gain confidence as a student and speaker. Being the center of attention was new for Winfrey, and school became a safe place where she could do her best and be recognized for her accomplishments. A defining moment in Winfrey's young life was her first trip to the library in Nashville. Today, Winfrey looks back on getting a library card as a pivotal moment, saying it was like being given citizenship. But she didn't just get a library card, she was also encouraged by her parents to write book reports about the books she checked out in addition to her homework. Winfrey didn't mind the extra work, and she thrived on her new identity as a good student and speaker.

Her father and stepmother celebrated Winfrey's speaking skills, and they took her to different churches all over the city to recite poems and scripture. Vernon Winfrey was incredibly proud of her and still remembers her talent at such a young age:

When she was nine years old and brought greetings to our church at large, I remember this poem, it was "Invictus," it was a pretty long speech and I thought that was a pretty big thing for her at that age, before the hordes of a couple hundred folk. And the way she gave her dissertation and people were shouting for joy.

Dark Times Ahead

Winfrey returned to Milwaukee for a summer visit with her mother and found a different life waiting for her

The Weight of "Invictus"

"Invictus" is a poem by William Ernest Henley. Written in 1875 and published in 1888, the poem focuses on themes of independence and perseverance—two themes that have come to define Oprah Winfrey.

Though she may not have understood the full weight of the words as she said them, lines like these must have left a lasting impression on Winfrey, who was about to experience great hardships at a young age and would need to embody the fearlessness described in the poem to meet her full potential:

> Out of the night that covers me,
>   Black as the pit from pole to pole,
> I thank whatever gods may be
>   For my unconquerable soul.
>
> In the fell clutch of circumstance
>   I have not winced nor cried aloud.
> Under the bludgeonings of chance
>   My head is bloody, but unbowed.
>
> Beyond this place of wrath and tears
>   Looms but the Horror of the shade,
> And yet the menace of the years
>   Finds and shall find me unafraid.
>
> It matters not how strait the gate,
>   How charged with punishments the scroll,
> I am the master of my fate,
>   I am the captain of my soul.

there. Her mother had moved into a larger apartment with her sister, Patricia, and their new baby brother, Jeffrey. Her mother continued to work long hours, but this left Winfrey plenty of time to read and look after her siblings. As the summer came to an end, Winfrey's father came to Milwaukee to get her before the school year started again. Though she loved her teachers and family in Nashville, she was afraid of displeasing her mother and refused to return.

While she continued to give speeches and recite stories and poems at every possible opportunity, Winfrey was very lonely. She still continued to excel in her studies, however. One of her middle school teachers at Lincoln Middle School noticed her gift for reading and

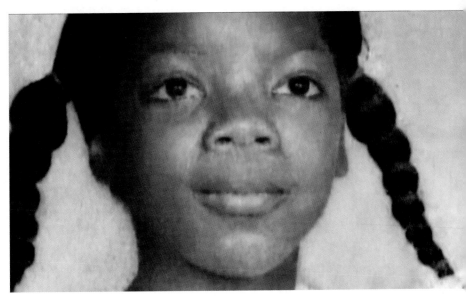

Winfrey's childhood was marked with tragedy and lack of stability, but her ability to beat the odds is part of her legacy.

helped her get into an all-white high school in nearby Glendale, Wisconsin. Though the Supreme Court ruled that **segregation** in schools was illegal, racism was still an issue in much of the United States. Many schools continued to be divided by race, either intentionally or because of the communities in which different races tended to live.

Trouble at Home

Though supported by her teachers in school, Winfrey and her siblings were often in the care of negligent babysitters at home. One night in 1963, while her mother was away, Oprah was abused by her cousin, who was supposed to be looking after her, her brother, and her sister. When she began crying, her cousin took her out for ice cream and told her not to tell anyone what he'd done.

These abuses became more frequent, and over the next few years, from the time Winfrey was ten to fourteen years old, other men in her family took advantage of her. There was no way to prepare for the devastating trauma that she endured during those years, and she responded by becoming rebellious and trying to run away from home. When she was fourteen years old, Winfrey found out she was pregnant.

Though she spent many months hiding her pregnancy, when the baby was born it became impossible to conceal her secret. Outraged, her mother—who had herself given birth to Oprah as a single, teen mother—took her to a **detention home**. Looking back on that time Winfrey has said in interviews, "I hid the pregnancy for seven months until the baby was born ... hiding that secret and carrying that shame blocked me in so many ways."

Luckily for Winfrey, the detention home was full, and they were not able to take her. Winfrey's mother took her back to Nashville to live with her father, where she was given a second chance. The baby had been born early and died within weeks of its birth. As her given name suggests, though, good things can come out of the darkest times:

> I remember being taken to the detention home when my mother was going to take me out of the house at fourteen ... and recognizing in that moment that I have been abused since I was nine years old ... and now pregnant as a result of that, and looking around the detention home at all of these girls who had been placed there for being "bad girls," and I remember having a moment thinking, Now I am officially a bad girl ... And after I gave birth, when that child died, my father said to me "This is your second chance, this is your opportunity to seize this opportunity and make something of your life." And I took that chance.

A Second Chance

It had been a very difficult five years for young Oprah Winfrey. She had been rebellious in Milwaukee, but her father would not stand for the same type of behavior when she returned to Nashville. He enforced a strict curfew and watched over Winfrey's studies. This guidance was exactly what she needed to excel.

From Winfrey's success in high school, nobody would ever guess how challenging her childhood had been. Her high school career seemed to be one victory after the next. With a dedication to learning and the support of her family, she continued to give speeches, enter competitions, and gain recognition. In 1970, Winfrey entered the Tennessee Elks Lodge speaking contest and won a four-year scholarship to Tennessee State University. While still reeling from this achievement, she was elected vice president of the student council after running with the slogan "Vote for the Grand Ole Oprah"—a play on the famous Tennessee music venue, the Grand Ole Opry.

Another life-changing moment presented itself when Winfrey and one other student were selected to represent the state of Tennessee at The White House Conference on Youth in Estes Park, Colorado. Like a snowball gaining mass as it rolls down a hill, one recognition of her work led to another. When Winfrey returned from her trip to Colorado, the local radio station, WVOL, asked her to come on the air to talk about her experience. A year later, they called on her again to represent the station in a local Miss Fire Prevention contest—a beauty pageant sponsored by the local firehouse.

Winfrey hesitated at first. She was confident giving speeches with her strong **oratory** skills, but she had never considered entering a beauty pageant. Furthermore, the contest would be full of young white girls. A black girl had never won the contest before.

Many years later, during an interview with her icon, anchorwoman Barbara Walters, Winfrey described how strange it felt to be on that stage. During the question and answer session at the beauty pageant, the contestants had been asked what careers they wanted to pursue.

With the promise of a full scholarship for college, Winfrey graduated from high school in 1971.

Inspired by seeing Barbara Walters on *The Today Show*, Winfrey answered that she wanted to be a broadcast journalist. It was a bold thing to say as a young black girl:

> *I am a little black girl standing on stage with all of these red-haired Miss Fire Prevention contestants, and because all of the other careers are taken ... I thought, Okay, I want to be Barbara Walters. Even just to say, "I want to be a journalist like Barbara Walters," was so off-putting to everybody.*

However off-putting that comment may have been, Winfrey still won the contest. And it wouldn't be long before she began living her dream of being a journalist.

The years of public speaking were starting to pay off. As she finished her senior year, Winfrey worked on the radio with WVOL as a part-time **newsreader**. She wasn't writing the stories she shared over the radio, but she gained invaluable experience delivering them to a large audience, and listeners noticed her skill.

Winfrey's career as a newswoman was taking off. With only one credit needed to graduate, she quit her college studies to focus on her career.

Winfrey graduated from high school in June of 1971 and prepared to study speech and drama at Tennessee State University with the full scholarship awarded from the Elks Lodge. To save money, she decided to live at home with her father and stepmother, while continuing to work part time at the radio station.

College promised to be a new land of opportunity where she could continue to learn and grow, but it was the opportunities outside of school that drew Winfrey's attention.

While speaking to the 2008 graduating class at Stanford University, Winfrey said:

> I never would have gotten my diploma at all, because ... I was short one credit. And I figured, I'm just going to forget it ... Because by that point, I was already on television. I'd been in television since I was nineteen and a sophomore. Granted, I was the only television anchor person that had an 11 o'clock curfew doing the 10 o'clock news.

As her career took off, Winfrey had less and less time to complete that final credit in order to graduate from college. It wasn't until years later, after she began hosting a show named after her, that Tennessee State University asked her to give a speech to their new graduates. She took her father's unrelenting advice to finish her degree so she could give the commencement speech as a graduate of Tennessee State.

CHAPTER TWO

The Road to Success

The first few years of Oprah Winfrey's career were a mix of victories and frustrations. As she grew unhappy with school and more interested in her career, new opportunities presented themselves. Winfrey was talented and was doggedly dedicated to pursuing professional success. At the same time, the country was undergoing big changes that helped propel her career forward.

Winfrey's success is thanks to a blend of her tireless hard work, charming TV personality, and willingness to take opportunities when they arise.

Making Her Own Way

One of Winfrey's greatest opportunities came in the form of a phone call that she received in the middle of a class during her sophomore year at college. Chris Clark, from Nashville's local news station, had gotten word from WVOL that they had a talented young newsreader interested in television. This was in the early 1970s, and American news outlets were only beginning to focus on diversity.

A combination of talent and being in the right place at the right time helped Winfrey make a very important leap in her career. She may be the most powerful woman in television today, but at that time she was nineteen and had no television experience. In the job interview, Clark asked Winfrey just two questions: "Can you run a camera, and can you write a news story?" She said yes, but what she meant was that she could learn.

This "little white lie" landed Winfrey her first television job. Most people would be nervous being on camera for the first time, but not Oprah Winfrey. Whether she realized it or not, she had been preparing for that job her entire life. Though she still had a lot of learning to do, Winfrey says being on the air was second nature to her. She said, "It felt like breathing. It felt like this is where I'm supposed to be."

Winfrey wasn't the only person who sensed her natural talent. Even as she was just getting started on the job, her new boss, Chris Clark, noticed that

"[Winfrey] had the magic to communicate on television … You just can't learn that. You can't develop that. You [got] it or you don't."

A Big Leap

Winfrey was performing well on the air but wasn't doing as well socially in school. She didn't participate in rallies or demonstrations with many of her classmates who were actively seeking racial equality through protesting. In her long string of successes, Winfrey hadn't felt the weight of **discrimination** that the other students must have felt. Her lack of support drove a wedge between her and her peers:

They all hated me—no, they resented me. I refused to conform to the militant thinking of the time … Everybody was angry for four years … Whenever there was any conversation on race, I was on the other side. Maybe because I never felt the kind of repression other black people are exposed to.

Though she had an excellent stage presence, it turned out she wasn't a great reporter. Despite her dreams of becoming a newswoman like Barbara Walters, Winfrey had a tendency to become too involved in her subjects to report the facts objectively. Because of this, she would often struggle to meet her deadlines. If she was reporting on an accident, for example, Winfrey spent all of her time

Even as she struggled to report *just the facts*, the skills Winfrey gained as she interviewed people became one of her greatest assets.

helping the people she reported on, rather than working on the assignment itself. Of her relentless goodwill, Chris Clark said, "It probably was very good she never got the message. Look at her today … She has **empathy** for people. She wouldn't be Oprah without that."

Despite her struggles to report on stories without bias or emotion, Winfrey had a winning television presence and was assertive enough to stand up for what she believed in. Former coworkers have told stories about Winfrey's willingness to take over when the job was not being done right. Once, during a **public service announcement (PSA)** for Black History Week, the crew felt the producer wasn't doing his job well. Winfrey took over. A coworker said, "She … told the cameraman what to do, and directed the segment herself … This girl knew what she wanted and was willing to do whatever she had to do to accomplish her goals."

Thanks to her strong presence both on camera and off, Winfrey began receiving job offers from around the country. The first offer came from Atlanta in 1975, but when the director of the station that was recruiting her left for another job in Philadelphia, Winfrey hesitated. Chris Clark offered her a $5,000 raise and talked her out of going. "I talked her out of it because she wasn't ready, and we didn't want to lose her," Clark said. Within a few years, she had another offer from Baltimore's local station, WJZ. This time her boss didn't try so hard to keep her in Nashville: "I called her in. 'Oprah, management has told me to talk you out of leaving. Have I tried to talk you out of it? Good. Now I think you should take the job. You're ready.'"

By all accounts, Winfrey had plenty of confidence. But Clark's support helped her take another big leap as she moved from home and began this new chapter in her life.

A Rough Start in Baltimore

Winfrey describes herself upon arriving in Baltimore as being "just as 'Beverly Hillbillies' as I could be." She may have still been a southern country girl at heart, but she quickly saw what she was up against in her new city.

To promote her as a new anchorwoman, the station ran an ad campaign asking, "What's an Oprah?" Her name was on the back of buses and on billboards, and was frequently discussed both on the radio and on television. While the local studio thought this was a great way to build attention for their new anchor, Winfrey was horrified that the uniqueness of her name was being made into a joke. In addition to feeling humiliated as the city struggled with her name, she felt there was no way to live up to the expectations of the advertisements. "When I arrived, people were expecting this big something." Winfrey said. "The buildup was so strong. And I'm just a colored girl with a lot of hair sitting next to Jerry Turner, and everybody's like, 'Whaaaaaaaaattttt? That's what an Oprah is?'"

Being hired as the station's only black woman presented its own slew of obstacles. She faced harassment and discrimination in ways that she had never before had to deal with. However frustrating, Winfrey does have fond memories of Baltimore: "It grew me into a real woman. I came in naive, unskilled, not really knowing anything about the business—or about life. And Baltimore grew me up."

Unfortunately, "growing up" meant facing discrimination based on her race and gender, as Winfrey fought to gain footing in a new, competitive job. In addition to the tasteless advertisements, she had the distinct feeling that her popular and experienced cohost, Jerry Turner, didn't want her there. Turner's animosity

Throughout her career, Winfrey has stood out in a field dominated by white men. Her success has helped motivate women and people of color to strive for their greatest potential despite the prejudices they may face.

toward Winfrey for sharing his spotlight was hardly concealed. He often tried to humiliate her, asking questions like, "What little college did you go to, again?" For the first time in her life, Winfrey was faced with being ashamed of where she came from.

After only seven months on the job, she was fired gracelessly on April 1, 1977. At first, Winfrey thought it was an April Fools' joke—but when her supervisor said they were going to put her on the morning cut-ins (a position with almost no air time), she was furious. It is to her credit that she didn't turn around and go back to Nashville. Winfrey's stay in Baltimore was marked by a number of struggles that demanded patience and strategy to overcome.

Over the next year that Winfrey spent at WJZ, she experienced defeats in nearly every way. She was sent to the newsroom where she was supposed to write copy—a job Winfrey herself admits was not her strength—and where she got very little time on camera. In addition to being demoted from the job she'd moved halfway across the country to do, Winfrey faced almost constant discrimination as a woman in a predominantly male field. Her supervisors would demand that she do favors for them, ranging from babysitting their kids to housing their girlfriends without asking for rent.

While her friends encouraged her to fight back and even to take those supervisors to court for discrimination, Winfrey worried that generating that level of attention would be the end of her career. To make it through this difficult time, she reminded herself that this was a temporary phase, and that she was destined for bigger and better things. She was so confident that Baltimore was just a stop along the way that she didn't even bother to learn the street names.

A Slow Climb

In addition to learning tough lessons about inequality in the workplace, Winfrey learned that even if she wanted a career in television, she didn't want to work in journalism. After taking blankets to a family she'd reported on when their house burned down, her supervisor threatened to fire her for getting personally involved in what should have been an objective story. Winfrey recognized the importance of reporting objectively so viewers would trust the station to report the truth, but she wanted to help people. She finally decided that journalism wasn't going to give her a chance to do what she needed to do. It's a good thing she figured it out, because her generosity is still what Winfrey is known for today. Winfrey's soft heart wasn't a benefit in the newsroom, but it has become a hallmark characteristic of her personality as an interviewer and **philanthropist**.

Realizing she needed to rethink her career, Winfrey accepted a cohosting position on a morning talk show, *People are Talking*, with Richard Sher. The switch from news anchor to talk-show host was one of the most important choices she would make in becoming the television personality we know today.

The new show gave Winfrey a chance to shine without the demand to report objectively. It turned out that talking was exactly what she did best. Furthermore, her cohost actually *wanted* to work with her.

Richard Sher was much more enthusiastic about working with Winfrey than Jerry Turner had been. Sher and his wife became Winfrey's close friends, and she would often stop by their house for dinner or to talk. She even had her own drawer in their kitchen for snacks and would sometimes just drop in for a few pretzels while out jogging.

Winfrey and Sher had a good relationship on *People are Talking*, as well. They learned to share screen time and included each other naturally in interviews, even if it took some getting used to.

However, Baltimore's TV critic, Bill Carter, was not a fan of the show. His review of the first show started with

Winfrey discovered her calling when she left the newsroom to join the talk show *People Are Talking*. What may have seemed like a small step would turn out to be a huge leap in the star's career.

"There was nothing much worth hearing—or seeing."
The show was criticized for being poorly paced "like
some sort of souped-up car with a rookie driver who
has never used a clutch before," and Richard Sher was
accused of "hogging air time with an ego that 'swallowed
up the cohost, the guests, and most of the furniture.'" By
the end of that horrible first review, only Winfrey was
commended for her performance.

The critics may have been harsh, but viewers loved it.

A Light At the End of the Tunnel

Though Winfrey's career was back on track, and she
began making progress in Baltimore, there was still room
for improvement. For example, though they started the
show together, Sher was making twice as much money
as Winfrey. According to Winfrey:

*I never really considered, or called myself, a feminist—but
I don't think you can be a woman living in this world and
not be. It was 1980, and I was getting paid $22,000 and
the guy I was co-anchoring with was getting paid $50,000.
So I went in to my boss and said, "He's getting paid a lot
more money than I am." And you know what my boss said?
"Why should you make that much money?" I said, "Because
we're doing the same job." He says, "I don't think so." So I
thought, Hm. I'll show you.*

A Brief History of Feminism

Women march for equality on Women's Day in 1977.

Women have been crusading for equality since the 1800s. **Feminism** is the belief that women are politically, socially, and economically equal to men. Over time, as women have come closer to true equality to men, the demands of feminism have changed. These phases are referred to as first-, second-, and third-wave feminism.

In 1847, Elizabeth Cady Stanton drafted the "Declaration of Sentiments," which states that "all men and women are created equal and endowed by their creator with certain inalienable rights." This document marked the official beginning of feminism, and it asked for basic rights, such as voting, owning property, and access to education. Wyoming was the first state in the union to allow women to vote in 1869. Across the country in Rochester, New York, Susan B. Anthony tried to vote, but was arrested and given a one hundred dollar fine.

Finally, in 1920 women were given the right to vote. More than one hundred years later, Betty Friedan began second-wave feminism when she wrote the best-selling book, *The Feminine Mystique*. The book claimed that media representations of women as homemakers refused to recognize the many other capabilities of women.

Throughout the 1960s and 1970s—just as Winfrey was beginning her career in broadcast journalism—women sought equal opportunities in the workplace. In 1963, women won the right to equal pay. All over the United States, women and minorities called for respect and a shot at the success that had historically been reserved for white males.

Third-wave feminism refers to social inequalities that persist despite the success women achieved in earlier crusades. Despite legislation that helped bridge the wage gap between men and women, women have had to continue working toward equal treatment and fair representation, both in the workplace and in the media.

Winfrey showed her boss and everyone else in Baltimore what she was worth when she got a job with *AM Chicago*, a poorly ranked morning show, in 1984. Within a year, the show was the highest ranked program in the city. In September of 1986, the show was renamed *The Oprah Winfrey Show*. It wasn't long before the show was **syndicated,** and people all over the country were tuning in to Winfrey's unique approach to celebrity interviews and important issues.

Winfrey's unequal pay in Baltimore was not the last time she would face discrimination as a woman or minority in television. Even as she gained national success, the demands on her to act as a representative for racial minorities and women became overwhelming. In an interview with *People* magazine shortly after her show became a national success, Winfrey lamented the pressure she felt to speak on behalf of all women and all African Americans all of the time:

> People feel you have to lead a **civil rights** movement every day of your life, that you have to be a spokeswoman and represent the race. I understand what they're talking about, but you don't have ... to do what other people want you to do ... I'm black. I'm a woman. I wear a size 10 shoe. It's all the same to me.

At only thirty-one years old, Winfrey relaxes in the studio of her very own talk show, *AM Chicago*, soon to be renamed in her honor. .

Her tireless refusal to be categorized by her race, gender, or traumatic past is part of her great success. Winfrey wasn't interested in being the most successful black women in the room, she was ready to become the most successful person of any race or gender in media across the country. Thanks to her skills as a businesswoman, Winfrey has become the most powerful female **media mogul** in the United States—and even one of the most influential women in the world.

Money-Saving Store Coupons Inside!

TV GUIDE

®

Aug. 26–Sept. 1
75¢

Oprah!
The Richest Woman on TV?

How she amassed her $250-million fortune

Page 2

0 714358

CHAPTER THREE

Becoming Oprah

Feeling that her time in Baltimore was coming to a close, Winfrey mentally began preparing for the next step. Her best friend, both when she was still living in Baltimore and today, Gayle King, was supportive but surprised by Oprah's fearlessness. King also worked in television, and the two often commiserated over the roadblocks they faced. In their Baltimore days together, King was constantly impressed with Winfrey's fortitude and sense of purpose.

When Winfrey learned that a position as a host was opening in Chicago, she immediately began putting together an **audition** tape to send to the station in

A long way from the farm in Mississippi, Oprah Winfrey became the richest woman on television.

hopes of getting an interview. She worked all night, splicing together clips from her show with Richard Sher and other television appearances. Perhaps to avoid the embarrassment she had faced upon first arriving in Baltimore, Winfrey's audition tape began with an explanation of the origin of her name.

Trial and Error

Oprah Winfrey moved to Chicago and began hosting *AM Chicago* in the spring of 1984. When she arrived, the show was poorly ranked, and she tried a little bit of everything to improve the ratings. Today, she describes her first shows as disastrous.

Nothing worked. Everything fell apart. I'm cooking—I don't cook. Certainly didn't cook then, and certainly not on a hotplate on TV ... It was just one wrong thing after another. It was a total mess, but I got through it. And came off thinking, You know, I should have asked them what the show was about.

She certainly figured it out, though. By the summer of 1984, Winfrey's charisma had made *AM Chicago* the most popular show in the city. She beat the former leading talk show, *Donahue*, and was a hit with the local crowd. Viewers were drawn to her easy manner and good nature. She and her agent negotiated a three-year contract. Far from the $22,000 she'd been making in Baltimore, her salary was now $230,000 a year with planned raises. Oprah had also been cast in a movie adaptation of the book *The Color Purple*. Her role in the film introduced her to a new audience outside of Chicago and daytime television. The book and film both illustrate the struggles of a young black woman as she learns to command respect and attention—both were themes Oprah Winfrey knew a lot about.

Big Changes

Winfrey's performance in *The Color Purple* was nominated for major awards, including an Academy Award, which honors achievements in the film industry, and a Golden Globe, which celebrates great work in television and movies. No one was asking, "What's an Oprah?" anymore.

Oprah Winfrey was becoming a household name in Chicago and receiving praise for her work, plus an ample paycheck. *The Oprah Winfrey Show* had even begun to win awards. In 1987, she won a Daytime **Emmy Award** for outstanding talk show. This recognition was enough for Winfrey—at least for a little while.

In the glow of success, she approached her **network** about getting more pay for the hardworking team that helped make her show possible. The response she got sounded eerily familiar: Why should they be paid more? They're all girls.

Winfrey points to that conversation as a defining moment in her career. Being told, once again, that women didn't need to be paid for their work made her ask how she could do more. As Winfrey was fighting for better pay for her female employees, she started hearing

The Oprah Winfrey Show began winning national awards, like this Daytime Emmy for Outstanding Talk or Service Show host, won in 1987.

that her agent was a "great guy" from the network that produced her show. While this seemed like a good thing at first, she began to question whether he was a good agent for her, or a good guy for the network. In order to realize her dream of taking more control of the show, Winfrey had to make a bold move. She fired her agent and took on a new lawyer, Jeff Jacobs, who was known for being very aggressive.

With Jacobs' legal assistance, the show gained a new name: *The Oprah Winfrey Show*. This new name not only allowed her to create the show in her image but gave it appeal outside of Chicago. Roger Ebert, an influential film critic, privately encouraged Oprah to consider **syndicating** the show so it would be available to a national audience. With her drive and her new lawyer's savvy, Winfrey achieved this goal. On September 8, 1986, *The Oprah Winfrey Show* aired across the country for the first time.

A Moment to Reflect

The night before the first national show, Winfrey began asking herself what the show could grow into and why she felt so compelled to do it. For a brief moment in the whirlwind her life had become, she was able to step back and think about what her role as a television personality meant. These questions led her to thinking about her role as an interviewer differently. She decided that her job wasn't just to ask famous people questions, it was to help people from all backgrounds tell their story so they could connect with others. That night she wrote in her journal: "Maybe going national was to help me realize that I have important work."

Actually, she didn't have to worry about asking famous people questions in her first few shows. Outside of Chicago, celebrities didn't care who she was. Her staff tried to lure a few different celebrities onto the show with the promise of expensive gifts, but with no luck. Finally, Winfrey said she wanted to do what she'd already been doing—interviewing ordinary people about their lives. The show gained recognition, and eventually it became easier to entice famous people to come onto the show, but Winfrey continued to talk to people from all walks of life about their experiences. Even after twenty-five years of *The Oprah Winfrey Show*, Oprah claims her favorite episodes are the ones in which she had unknown guests who experienced a moment of self-discovery and improved their lives as a result.

Going All The Way

Beyond thinking about what she needed to do to be a great on-camera host, working with Jeff Jacobs reshaped the way Winfrey imagined her role off camera. She didn't just want to own the content and creative direction; she wanted the power to pay her employees what she thought was fair. With help from her new lawyer, Winfrey negotiated the purchase of her show, as well as the studios where it was made and a portion of the company that distributed it. She named her new production company Harpo Studios, Harpo being "Oprah" spelled backwards. There was a lot of money in that unique name, and Oprah Winfrey has continued to capitalize on it over the course of her career.

Many people couldn't believe that she would take such a large risk. She had fired an agent who secured a huge salary for her and found a new agent and lawyer who had helped her take the show to a national market. But buying the show would mean putting all of those gains on the line. Winfrey responded, "I had to get rid of that slave mentality. That's where Jeff [Jacobs] came in. He took the ceiling off my brain."

Winfrey was discovering what the early pioneers in the feminist movement had realized: if she owned the show, no one could own her. Winfrey stated:

What we did with the platform of The Oprah Winfrey Show *was to validate women, to say you matter. You matter if you have been divorced. You matter if you have been abused. You are not your circumstances, you are what is possible for you. That was my initial* **intention** *that I stated on the very first day of* The Oprah Winfrey Show, *and what I realize is that is exactly what we did*

In 1993, Winfrey proved her big risk had paid off when she announced a groundbreaking opportunity— an interview with the world's most famous musician. Her interview with Michael Jackson was a monumental event because it was the first one he'd given in fourteen years. With 90 million viewers, the hour-and-a-half long special was the most watched television interview in history. Winfrey says of entering Jackson's famous home, "We are coming in the gates of Neverland, and

Winfrey has had the opportunity to interview countless celebrities, like pop legend Michael Jackson, who had not given an interview in fourteen years when he agreed to speak to her in 1993.

it's like a moment in *The Wizard of Oz*. It was literally like going to see the wizard. We couldn't believe it. I felt like a kid."

Winfrey had seen the Jackson Five in concert when she was still a teenager in Nashville and was as excited about the five famous brothers as any other teenage girl. True to her nature, even while talking to one of pop music's greatest legends, she remained calm and open, joking that she'd had a crush on one of his older brothers.

Though Jackson is famous for his music, there were also many rumors circulating about him at that time, and Winfrey asked him probing questions about difficult parts of his life. After opening with a few soft questions about his musical influences, she jumped into more personal questions about his abusive childhood and plastic surgery. Many people also thought he had deliberately bleached his skin to be white, and they accused him of being ashamed of being African American.

Although he'd refused to give an interview for over a decade, Jackson was calm with Winfrey. He admitted to having low self-esteem about his looks and continuing to suffer emotionally from his father's abuse. For the first time, Jackson talked about having a rare condition that made areas of his skin extremely pale.

This was a breakthrough moment on television. Michael Jackson had never opened up to a television personality before, and no one was more qualified to interview the pop star on these topics than Winfrey.

The Private Life of a Star

Oprah Winfrey's fame (and fortune) continued to grow as her show grew in popularity. Through her show she was able to meet some of her own idols, like Barbara Walters and Michael Jackson. Some stars came on the show many times over the course of their careers. She conducted star-studded interviews with celebrities like Tom Cruise and Mariah Carey, and gave their fans a rare glimpse into their lives and personalities.

People tuned into *The Oprah Winfrey Show* for news about their favorite celebrities, but Winfrey had become a celebrity herself. People wanted to know all about their favorite talk-show host as well.

One of Winfrey's strengths as a television personality is her openness. As people learned more about her, she came to seem like a close friend that everyone could tune into from all over the world. On her very first national show, she enthusiastically welcomed her studio audience and viewers all over the country by yelling, "Welcome to the very first *Oprah Winfrey Show*!" As soon as the moment of excitement passed, she immediately began making jokes about looking for a husband and dieting.

Winfrey used her own struggles and desires to relate to her guests and audience. She shattered the expectations of her viewers by incorporating them into her show. In a move that was highly unusual for talk shows at the time, Winfrey would walk the aisles taking questions from the studio audience. To further blend

Winfrey's relationship with Stedman Graham has been a recurring topic on her show as well as in the tabloids.

into her own audience, she would make jokes about her personal life and admit to her own insecurities. Because so much of her life did become public knowledge, her guests trusted her with their own life stories.

As with many celebrities, the more people knew about Winfrey from watching her show, the more they wanted to know about her life off-camera. Her fans were thrilled when, after a year of living single in Chicago, Winfrey began dating Stedman Graham. This gave fans something to read about in tabloids— and it gave Winfrey new material for her show. Even today, her weight and her thirty-year relationship with Graham come up in her interviews as well as in celebrity gossip columns.

This gossip about her life feeds into her image as an ordinary person with the same struggles and hopes as her viewers. Winfrey has said that after interviewing thirty thousand people, from all circumstances and economic backgrounds, everyone had one thing in common: they all wanted validation. Everyone, Winfrey says, from those grieving the loss of a loved one to a star like Beyoncé, wants to be heard and understood. Winfrey has made helping others find their voice a mission in her lifelong career in television and media:

> I knew during the Oprah show ... in our culture we value fame. So I always understood that was the basis for me being known in the world, because people wouldn't be able to hear you unless you came with some ... swagger. But I also understand that that was just the foundation to be heard, but there was a lot more to be said. All of us have a limited time here—the real question is who are you, and what do you want to do with it?

Despite being the queen of her profession, Winfrey has long relied on a surprising approach to interviewing. She never prepares questions in advance. Her method might seem risky. Many people would get nervous or freeze up while interviewing their favorite actor or musician, but Winfrey sees her unusual approach as a strength. It is part of what helps her be an active listener. Rather than worrying about how prepared *she* looks to her audience, she dedicates her full attention to her guest. By allowing those on her show to lead the conversation, she helps them satisfy their need to be heard.

Because Winfrey is the heart and soul of her show, it has changed over time, just like its host. While her refusal to write questions in advance never faltered, she began expanding her subject matter. Winfrey featured a wide variety of people on the show, from psychologists to a religious group that runs its own ranch. She interviewed her guests on topics ranging from heartache to heart disease and somehow made them accessible to everyone.

Eventually, the show expanded so much it could not be contained by its one-hour time slot. Winfrey decided it was time to expand.

A Not-So-Fresh Start

After twenty-five years on the air, Winfrey ended her show in 2011. Shutting down *The Oprah Winfrey Show* was a huge decision for the star. After all, it wasn't just her paycheck that would be affected, but all of her employees' paychecks as well. The show had also become a large part of her identity. Winfrey says of her decision to end the show in 2011, "I got through my time in Baltimore because I knew that wasn't *it*. Twenty-five years later in Chicago, I had that same feeling, that *this isn't it*."

In the January 2011 issue of *O, The Oprah Magazine*, Winfrey admitted to being afraid of what the future would hold. She considered taking a year off, spending time with friends, or going on a cruise, but her friends warned against a life of ease and luxury. Oprah had worked nearly every day of her life with the mission of making the world a better place. She listened to her friends' warning and realized what she'd spent so many years telling her viewers was true for her, too: she was her mission, not her show. Winfrey knew she had to take on a new challenge.

No longer content to own the highest-rated daytime talk show in America (and its production company, distributor, and a magazine named after her), she founded her own network, aptly titled the Oprah Winfrey Network (OWN). Owning a network would allow Winfrey to expand in new directions and create multiple shows. In many ways, her career was beginning all over again.

Winfrey partnered with Discovery Communications to build the Oprah Winfrey Network. Given her many other successes, it may come as a surprise that Winfrey's cable network was not an overnight sensation. In fact, unforeseen obstacles and negative reviews marked the first year.

Forbes magazine reports that Discovery and Winfrey poured a combined 500 million dollars into the network to keep it afloat through that first tumultuous year. Discovery had looked forward to the partnership, because they planned to replace their Health Channel with the new OWN brand. The Discovery Health Channel had been floundering, and they hoped Winfrey would bring the same magic to the channel that she'd brought to *Chicago AM* so many years before.

Bumps in the Road

To everyone's surprise, what Winfrey had learned about producing a single hour-long show didn't translate to running an entire network with programming twenty-four hours a day. In the network's first six months, Oprah was in the midst of one of the busiest periods in her life. Still wrapping up her famous show and fielding media attention for the decision, she was largely absent from the network that bore her name. OWN had come up with a smattering of entertainment in the form of one-off documentaries and what Peter Hamilton, a cable programming advisor, called "Oprah 'change the world' shows." Of that early rough start, Hamilton says, "They didn't really grasp that they needed series and hits that

Gayle King, Winfrey's longtime best friend, interviews her about the OWN network on *CBS This Morning*.

went beyond the traditional Oprah brand." That is, OWN needed something that would keep people coming back week after week, not just for a single movie they were interested in, but for a whole cast of characters viewers could invest in.

Looking back, Winfrey says she had to talk herself out of the darkness of the network's early shortcomings. "What did [I] expect would happen? [I was] going to end the *Oprah* show, go on a little cruise, and then step in and everything was going to be fine?"

In April of 2012, she spoke about the challenges of running a network on *CBS This Morning*. She said if she had known how difficult it would be, she might not have ever done it. When the cohosts, Charlie Rose and Gayle

King, asked what she would have done differently, she immediately said she would have waited. "[We launched] when we weren't really ready ... because [we'd said we] were going to do it. It's like having a wedding when you know you're not ready."

One headline in *USA Today* read, "Oprah Winfrey isn't quite holding her OWN." For a self-made billionaire who had overcome every variety of obstacle, that line struck particularly hard.

Holding Her OWN

Winfrey knew that she couldn't be the entire channel. She came to a sudden realization: "This channel can't be based upon me. It has to be based upon my philosophy and my ideas."

After a conversation with the CEO of Discovery, David Zaslav, Winfrey—and OWN—changed her tune. Though it had been a tough start, it was time for the team to step up to the plate and learn from their mistakes. They set about developing a new line of programming. Realizing that they needed to focus on series that would keep people tuning in week after week, the OWN team secured a contract with actor and director Tyler Perry. His first show with the network, *The Haves and the Have Nots*, quickly became the channel's most viewed show.

By July of 2012, OWN began making back their investment. Winfrey was cast in a new film, *The Butler*, and the headlines were looking a lot better.

CHAPTER FOUR

The Midas Touch

I n the 1970s, talk shows featured celebrity guests and played it safe with their subject matter. There was never any question as to who was the most important person in the room, and the audience was there to support that vision. But when Oprah Winfrey began having ordinary people on her show and made herself a part of the audience, she broke down barriers. By walking in the aisles to ask the audience questions and by sharing her own experiences, Winfrey blurred the lines. The message she constantly drove home to her viewers was that everyone—whether a celebrity or not— has the same needs and worries.

Winfrey's success is contagious, and she has built a legacy around sharing it with those in need.

Television As We Know It

In 1998, a professor of linguistics, Deborah Tannen, wrote about Oprah's revolutionary approach to being a talk-show host for *Time* magazine:

> *Winfrey saw television's power to blend public and private ... Like a family member, it sits down to meals with us and talks to us in the lonely afternoons. Grasping this paradox, Oprah exhorts viewers to improve their lives and the world. She makes people care because she cares. That is Winfrey's genius and will be her legacy.*

Winfrey's show took to the high road. Her deliberate focus on self-improvement, positive thinking, and charity set it apart from everything else on television. She found a way to both satisfy a growing need in her American audience, and to recreate that need. Her unique approach was revolutionary, and over time became the template others tried to follow. Many of her guests went on to host their own shows and modeled them after the example she set.

Winfrey's far-reaching influence is referred to by many in the media as "the Oprah effect." Janice Peck, a cultural researcher at the University of Colorado, writes that Winfrey's promise of self-transformation matters to her audience because this belief is so firmly rooted in America's own history. Winfrey's struggle with poverty and her dogged journey to the top is a realization of the classic American dream. Her ability to overcome adversity—combined with her tendency to promote underdog stories like her own—satisfies the hope many Americans have for themselves. Whether the obstacle is money, gender, race, sexual orientation, or abuse, Winfrey taught an entire generation that anything is possible with the right attitude.

Life Lessons

Always dreaming big, Winfrey again asked herself in the mid-1990s what the show could do that it wasn't already doing. Her ability to relate to everyone—from her famous guests to her audience members—was the building block of her success as a talk-show host. But then a few unsettling interviews on *Oprah* caused her to reconsider the direction the show was going, and she found that she still had lessons to learn.

Perhaps one of Winfrey's most challenging interviews was in the 1990s with the Ku Klux Klan (KKK), a group known for its long history of racism. As a black woman, she felt the challenge would teach listeners about the dangers of racial hatred. Experience had shown her that sometimes the greatest rewards come from the most difficult situations. She admits that she also hoped to use the interview to show her interviewees that race is a poor basis for a belief system—clearly, she thought, they would see during the interview that she wasn't so bad.

But the interview didn't go smoothly. During the commercial breaks she noticed the Klan members signaling to each other. Rather than feeling empowered by the interview, Winfrey realized she had given this group of men a national platform for their ideas about race—an agenda she not only didn't agree with, but which was directly damaging her and the people she wanted to support. They were using her huge viewership to recruit new members. She made the decision never to do a show like that again. That is, never to allow the show, which had been built upon the idea of inclusivity and empowerment, to be used to promote principles she didn't believe in. She wouldn't let *herself* be used again, either.

At that time, **confrontational television** was becoming popular. Confrontational television is a format that brings real people on a public show to unveil big secrets to their families. Usually these secrets are hurtful and dramatic. Winfrey felt these shows were tacky—she didn't want to make money on the pain of others, and she tried to avoid letting *The Oprah Winfrey Show* move in that direction. Yet, just after the show with the KKK, Winfrey found herself interviewing a couple struggling in their marriage. In the middle of the interview, the husband told his wife—and the entire world—that he was going to have a child with another woman. The look of humiliation on the wife's face made Winfrey feel terrible. That moment solidified for her that she would never do another episode like that.

Winfrey meets with the producers of *The Oprah Winfrey Show* to discuss the show's future.

In response to these two difficult interviews Winfrey met with her producers and said she was not going to be used by television. Instead, she told them, she was going to use television to make the world a better place. She wanted each episode moving forward to have an intention, or goal, and to be constructed around that goal:

> We were so driven to do and be the best. But after a while, those goals became empty for me. I'd think, So we're number one—now what? I was caught up in a whirlwind of trying to make every appearance and please the critics, the world, everybody. And I felt disconnected from myself ... what mattered was not just performing on TV but using the power of television to influence others for good, to help people see their potential and reconnect with themselves.

A New "Oprah"

The Oprah Winfrey Show became known for being hopeful and energetic. It was exactly this positivity that allowed her to take on difficult issues without alienating her audience. While getting out of journalism had allowed her to discover her voice, her early training in seeking out a story and learning the facts hadn't left her.

Winfrey engaged everyone on her show—from guest to audience member to at-home viewer. The show invited people to consider some of the most challenging issues of our time in a safe and accepting environment. Over time, Winfrey turned her approach to running the show—to have a positive goal and see it through—into the basis of *The Oprah Winfrey Show* itself. She said:

> *I live by the third law of physics … which is, for every action there is an equal and opposite reaction. I know that what I'm thinking, and therefore act on, is going to come back to me … just like gravity, like what goes up comes down. So I don't do anything without being fully clear about why I intend to do it. Because the intention is going to determine the result. And that is the secret to why we were number one all those years.*

Winfrey's contributions extend beyond the effect she had on the format of the daytime genre. *The Oprah Winfrey Show* enjoyed remarkable success as entertainment—but it was not what the show did for Winfrey that spurred her on, but what she could do with the show. She set out with the intention of validating women and their experience, and in doing so made enormous strides for gender and racial equality. She was a role model for women and minorities who needed to see what was possible beyond the struggle of their individual situations.

Winfrey helped those less fortunate than her to improve their idea of their own potential, while showing those traditionally in power—straight, middle-class, white men—that there was room at the table for others. She normalized seeing women and people of color in positions of power. That was an especially rare sight when the show started in the early 1980s.

Though she shunned political rallies and marches in her college years, in her later years, Oprah Winfrey led one of the largest marches for equality in the world every single week by simply being herself.

Taking on the Issues

Beyond tackling big **social issues**, Winfrey wanted her viewers to take on the issues that held them back in their own lives. Whether it was a weakness for cake or fear of failure, *The Oprah Winfrey Show* sought to make people more forgiving of one another and themselves. By taking on unpopular topics under the mantra "live your best life," Winfrey invited people to face their challenges head-on.

Winfrey opened her first national show with a quip about her thighs, and for the next twenty-five years, viewers tuned in to her lifelong struggle with diet and exercise. Through her show and magazine, Winfrey advocated for healthy lifestyle choices like jogging and eating well. When Winfrey started working with Bob Greene, a personal trainer, she sent a signal to the rest of the world to think about healthy living.

Winfrey's message about healthy living extended beyond watching her weight. In 2003, she aired a special on fistula in Ethiopia. Fistula is a condition suffered by women who give birth at a very young age. Without proper medical treatment, these women suffer abnormalities and are often shunned by their families. Before her special episode on the topic, few people in America were aware of the problem. When Winfrey brought the issue to light, she was able to raise $2.2 million for the cause almost instantly.

Part of her mission to improve people's lives also includes working toward a healthier planet. In the early 2000s, the idea of bringing reusable bags to the grocery store was still new. People were starting to ask where the one hundred billion plastic shopping bags used in the United States every year go—especially when they take one thousand years to degrade. When Winfrey featured eco-friendly bags on her show, however, millions of viewers instantly got on board. In the past ten years, laws have been passed across the United States to remove plastic bags from grocery stores and retailers.

Jane Elliott's Experiment

In 1992, Winfrey invited Jane Elliott, a diversity expert, to join her on the show. The entire episode was composed around a social experiment, or a research project with real people, to see how they would react to a given situation. Jane Elliott's particular experiment focused on eye color.

The audience of that episode was divided into two groups: those who had blue eyes and those with brown eyes. The blue-eyed audience members were made to wait for a long time in a hot room without chairs, while the brown-eyed group was taken to a special room with free snacks and drinks. The brown-eyed audience members were then led into the studio in front of the tired crowd of blue-eyed audience members.

Throughout the show, Elliott insisted that brown-eyed people were smarter and more deserving than blue-eyed people. When accused of being blue-eyed herself, she said she'd learned to "act brown-eyed." The blue-eyed audience members were offended and angry. Because most blue-eyed people are Caucasian, many of the blue-eyed audience members had not been discriminated against because of their race. The brown-eyed group, on the other hand, included a wider variety of ethnicities, and many had experienced discrimination in some form.

After a few minutes of debate, the audience realized the show was really about racial discrimination. Once they realized Winfrey and her guest didn't really believe blue-eyed people were less valuable than brown-eyed people, the audience was able to have an open conversation about prejudice.

Personal trainer Bob Greene became a regular feature in Winfrey's life when she took on healthy living as one of her causes.

Oprah Changed Everything

Thanks to the long-running success of her show and her wide-reaching influence, *Forbes* magazine ranked Winfrey as the twelfth most powerful woman in the world. Part of what earns Winfrey that status is that she is constantly finding ways to share that power with others. Rather than believing the only way to stay on top is by keeping others down, she found that by lifting others up she gained success herself. *The Oprah Winfrey Show* often dedicated time to discuss the work of new thinkers and artists. This generosity on her show paved the way for others to enjoy victories in many career fields outside of television. Winfrey's approval has become so meaningful to her fan base that her **endorsement** has the power to launch others' careers as well.

Some have referred to Winfrey's contagious success as the Midas touch, referring to the Greek myth about a king who turned everything he touched to gold. When Winfrey agreed to endorse Weight Watchers, for example, the company's value more than doubled in just one day. Many of the books she has featured on the show or in her book club have become best sellers. Even doctors and chefs who have come on her show as guests have gone on to create their own shows, such as Dr. Phil and Rachael Ray.

The publishing industry has also changed in the wake of Winfrey's on-air book club. Because her book club often features memoirs that cover the same difficult subjects that her show did, memoir has become a more popular genre. Publishers have sought out books that would be a good fit for the book club because Winfrey's approval has such a profound effect on sales. Bookstores sometimes feature displays of books that she has chosen for the club, while librarians have taken to recommending books similar to those she selected.

Winfrey continues lending her Midas touch to the people and things she believes in. A long-running Oprah tradition is to open the holiday season with a list of her favorite things. In 2015, those things ranged from book sets of classic novels to a box of twenty-four nail polish colors. While the list, which appears annually in *O* magazine, is meant as a gift guide, it is also an enormous boost for each of the companies featured. Winfrey's endorsement is as good as gold. The world witnessed exactly how powerful Winfrey's support really is when Weight Watchers saw their value go up 100 percent in just one day following her endorsement.

CHAPTER FIVE

On a Mission

O prah Winfrey is known for her philanthropy, or charity, for less fortunate people all over the world. She has made giving an important part of her legacy and identity.

Sharing the Wealth

In 2015, *Forbes* magazine estimated that Winfrey's assets were worth $3.2 billion, making her the 211th richest person, and the only African-American billionaire, in the world. Having so much wealth has made it possible for Winfrey to also be one of the most generous people on

Known for her philanthropy, Oprah has given generously to many causes all over the world.

earth. As much as her personality, Winfrey's boundless charity has kept her relevant throughout the last thirty years of her career. Beyond helping to promote artists and products on the show, she was also generous with her audience. Some of the most lavish gifts she gave her audience include houses, cars, weekend trips, and even cash.

While she struggled to finish college herself, it wasn't because she didn't value learning. Winfrey gives to many different causes, but education is at the top of her list. By 2012, Winfrey had given roughly four hundred million dollars to education. Her generosity and support has meant more than one million dollars in donations to charter schools and mentor programs all over the country. She's given ten million dollars to A Better Chance, which strives to make college more accessible to students of color. Her many donations have helped at least four hundred students at Moore College, a school for women in the arts. Her greatest contribution, however, is undoubtedly the forty million dollars she donated to found a school in South Africa.

Winfrey has also donated enormous sums to the arts, both in Chicago, where she made her great leap into stardom, and all around the United States. For instance, she has given millions to the Smithsonian's National Museum of African American History and Culture and the National Underground Railroad Freedom Center.

Education For the Future

The Oprah Winfrey Leadership Academy for Girls, a school for grades eight through twelve in South Africa, is one of Winfrey's most ambitious philanthropic projects. It took years of working closely with South African leaders in education to make that dream a reality.

Winfrey says she was having tea with Nelson Mandela, the former president of South Africa, when he told her that education was the key to ending poverty. Winfrey agreed, saying she had been thinking about building a school in Africa. Mandela immediately called the Minister of Education to join them for a meeting. "I really thought one day I would build the school," Winfrey has joked since. "I didn't mean *that* day."

The school opened in January of 2007 with its first class of eighth-grade girls. The school continued to add one grade each year as the girls advanced, until the first class graduated in 2011. Located on fifty-two acres in a small town outside Johannesburg, the boarding school offers girls free tuition, uniforms, and meals. The girls are selected for the program based on their academic ability and their need—many of the young women come from impoverished homes or traumatic pasts.

Mashadi Kekana, a graduate of the academy who went on to attend Wellesley College in Massachusetts, said of her arrival at the school, "Most of us had never been away from our families. We came to school with different languages, beliefs, religious practices, mind-sets, and experiences."

Winfrey regularly reminds the girls, whom she calls her "daughters," of a quote by Martin Luther King Jr.: "My young friends, doors are opening to you—doors of opportunities that were not open to your mothers and fathers—and the great challenge facing you is to be ready to face these doors as they open." In 2011, 71 young women from difficult backgrounds graduated with bright futures: 100 percent of the class had been accepted to college and 10 percent of the girls were moving to attend schools in the United States. Winfrey said:

> In the beginning, I think we had teachers who were like, "Oh, the girls, they come here disadvantaged." So we've eliminated that word "disadvantaged," because disadvantaged allows other people to look at you like you have some kind of disease, and they lower their expectations for what you can be. I said, "Nobody has a disadvantaged brain. Nobody is here with a disadvantaged mind. Nobody has a disadvantaged spirit."

When asked why this project has been so much more successful than others like it, Winfrey said that there *are* no other programs like it. She said many similar programs view the people they are trying to help as "less than" the people helping them. This creates an environment where those in need cannot learn to be self-

After a talk with former South African President Nelson Mandela, Winfrey founded the Oprah Winfrey School for Girls in South Africa.

reliant, so when they leave the program, they return to the circumstances they came from.

Winfrey's commitment and enthusiasm for helping these young girls continues beyond high school. That's why she started the Oprah Winfrey Leadership Academy Foundation, which supports her graduating academy students financially as they pursue college. As Oprah often points out, it's not all about the money—though the money certainly helps. To help the girls emotionally and academically, the academy also makes sure the girls have mentors as they leave the safety of the boarding school and enter the real world. Of course, the girls also have each other. At her graduation, Kekana said, "We came to the academy in 2007 with a myopic view of the world. But Mom-Oprah showed us that we're not just girls—we're girls who have greater purpose."

Why Africa?

According to the Brookings Institute, a nonprofit organization that conducts independent research, there is reason for concern about sub-Saharan Africa's education systems. "Under the current model," the Brookings Institute reports, "61 million children will reach adolescence without the basic skills needed to lead successful and productive lives."

There are many historical and cultural factors that play into Africa's struggle to meet growing demands for education, especially for girls. Often schools are far from students' homes and traveling long distances alone can be dangerous for women and girls. Poverty is also an obstacle in obtaining an education. Though the national or local government may cover tuition, parents often cannot afford uniforms or books. There are other, less obvious, costs of sending a child to school as well, such as losing help in agricultural work or around the home.

Nelson Mandela was on to something when he told Oprah that education was the key to relieving the issue of poverty in Africa. In their study, the Brookings Institute found that "the percentage of adults with less than two years of education show the disadvantages that poor, rural students face in accessing education in comparison to their rich and urban counterparts."

The Angel Network

Winfrey started The Angel Network almost by accident. In 1997, she asked her viewers to donate their spare change to help send 150 students from The Girls & Boys Club of America to college. She had such a positive response that she called on her viewers again, nearly ten years later. In 2005, Oprah asked viewers to donate their time to help build homes with Habitat for Humanity after Hurricane Katrina devastated parts of Texas, Mississippi, Louisiana, and Alabama. So many donations came in that Oprah founded The Angel Network to properly distribute the funds.

The Angel Network's mission was to enable individuals to act on opportunities to make a difference in their own communities. To drive this point home, Oprah once gave everyone in her studio audience one thousand dollars with instructions to use the money to help others. Between the gifts of 150,000 donors and her own contribution, The Angel Network gave out $80 million in aid over nearly a decade, before closing in 2010.

A House and a Home

Habitat for Humanity is an organization that helps low-income communities—and those affected by natural disasters—by working with volunteers to build homes. The organization takes on all kinds of building projects, sometimes tearing down old homes that are run-down or unsafe. When Habitat for Humanity workers find parts of a house that are still in good shape, they rescue them from demolition and sell them. This is helpful for people who don't have the money to buy things new at home-improvement stores. Habitat makes used light fixtures, doors, and building materials available to people who need them while also keeping those items out of landfills.

When Hurricane Katrina hit the Gulf Coast region in August of 2005, an estimated 1,800 people died and 550,000 homes were destroyed. Many survivors of the hurricane had to relocate to Houston after Katrina because the event had destroyed so much of the Louisiana coast. When rebuilding began in New Orleans, the cost of living increased by nearly 50 percent in just a few years. Many of the city's low-income population had to leave their homes, not just because they had been washed away, but because they couldn't afford to come back.

Where and how to rebuild was an urgent concern. Through Habitat for Humanity, many volunteers were able to help in the rebuilding effort. Former President Jimmy Carter, along with five thousand volunteers, got involved in Habitat for Humanity's Operation Home Delivery. This program focuses on delivering all the necessary building materials to construct a safe, simple home in a short period of time.

Winfrey's donation of fifteen million dollars helped build a small neighborhood outside of Houston. With the help of her viewers, who gave time and money to

Hurricane Katrina devastated the Gulf Coast region of the United States, destroying homes and displacing thousands of families.

facilitate the project, Habitat for Humanity was able to build sixty-five new homes. Winfrey also started the Angel Network gift registry so viewers could donate household items like lamps, furniture, and appliances. Matthew McConaughey, an actor, and Roger Clemens, a baseball player, worked together to build a playground in the neighborhood. The community of sixty-five houses was named Angel Lane.

Many of those who were selected to live in the new community were originally from New Orleans. Some had come to Houston to be with family, while others simply had nowhere else to go.

Long-Term Solutions

Winfrey had given the hurricane survivors the opportunity to start a new life, but she couldn't give them the new life itself. The criteria for applying to live in one of the new houses were simple but strict. Potential residents had to prove that they were working and were able to afford four hundred dollars a month for their house payments. They also had to be able to work on building their new home, and donate three hundred hours of labor to the project.

By volunteering with Habitat for Humanity in the construction of their homes, the new residents invested in the success of their community. They built their houses alongside their new neighbors and literally helped each other rebuild their lives after the storm.

When they applied to move into the new homes, potential residents didn't know that Winfrey was behind the project. Habitat for Humanity screened applicants and gave interviews. When the final families had been selected, they were told to meet at a local high school. Winfrey wanted to know that the people who moved in wanted to be there, and that they could afford to stay. Ten years later, sixty of the original sixty-five families still live in those homes. The majority of those who left were homesick and returned to Louisiana.

Angel Lane was just the beginning, though. Winfrey's mission was to put two hundred and fifty families displaced by the disaster into new homes. All across the devastated coastal region, Winfrey and Habitat for Humanity worked together on "blitz builds"—building as many as ten houses in a single week.

Winfrey's charity was contagious, and generous gifts poured in from viewers and celebrities. The rock band, Bon Jovi, donated one million dollars. Actress Eva Longoria and Tony Parker, a basketball player for the San Antonio Spurs, donated fifty thousand dollars to build a home for one of the displaced families. NBA star Kevin Garnett gave one of the largest contributions to Winfrey's project. He offered to pay for a new home to be built every month for two years, costing roughly $1.2 million. A host of celebrities gave to the cause in other ways as well. Actors Julia Roberts and George Clooney sent food and clothing, while Brad Pitt contributed to construction efforts.

Next Steps

While there have been trickle-down effects from Hurricane Katrina, much of the coast has been rebuilt in the last ten years. In Africa, The Oprah Winfrey Leadership Academy for Girls has been going strong since 2007, constantly expanding and gaining support. So what is Winfrey doing now?

When *The Oprah Winfrey Show* reached its final episode, The Angel Network also closed its doors. This wasn't because Oprah had lost interest in giving. It was quite the opposite. Since that final episode in 2011,

Winfrey has built an entire network around being charitable to others as well as to oneself—and this approach has been incredibly successful. As of 2015, the Oprah Winfrey Network is available to over 70 percent of all American households with a television.

Oprah Lends a Hand in Politics

Even politicians have benefited from Winfrey's Midas touch. In 2008, the presidential election was very close. Winfrey supported Barack Obama on that first campaign for office. Craig Garthwaite, a Northwestern University professor, studied the effects of Winfrey's endorsement of Obama. He estimates that her support won Obama about one million votes and may have made all the difference.

Winfrey joined Barack and Michelle Obama on the campaign trail in 2007. It is estimated that much of President Obama's public support stemmed from her endorsement.

Outside of her praise for Obama, Winfrey has endorsed few politicians. Those she has supported have been special cases or individuals that she was especially interested in seeing succeed. One such politician was Cory Booker, the mayor of Newark, New Jersey. Winfrey hosted a fundraiser for his campaign for the state senate. Prior to her endorsement, she interviewed him and opened by asking if he had plans to run for president. His answer proved why he is exactly the sort of politician Oprah Winfrey would support:

> *There have only been forty-five people ... that have been president of the United States. That's a terrible thing to hang your life on, that's your victory or success. Let [my success] be measured by my own barometer ... and my ability to make a difference in the lives of people.*

With Winfrey's support, it comes as no surprise that Booker has since gone on to serve in the United States Senate.

Winfrey's last big endorsement was for a Stanford University senior, Michael Tubbs. Tubbs was only twenty-one years old and not yet out of college when he began his campaign for Stockton City Council in Stockton, California. The *Stockton Record* reported that Tubbs had met Winfrey at a luncheon when she visited Stanford. Winfrey wanted to know more about this ambitious student and the struggles facing his beloved hometown. "She looked at me and said, 'How old are you?'" Tubbs recalled. "She kept coming back to Stockton. [She said:] 'Tell me about the city.' I told her about the homicides, how the city is broke."

Tubbs may be young, but he boasts impressive accomplishments. He has interned at The White House and is the Executive Director of The Phoenix Scholars, a program that helps mentor low-income students as they enter college. In addition to his successes, there's something else that drew Winfrey's attention. Like Winfrey, Tubbs was born to a teen mom in an unsafe neighborhood and has a lifelong love of public speaking. Tubbs grew up reciting Bible passages in front of his church congregation. The young politician even traveled to South Africa to help underserved communities there. He was a natural fit for Winfrey's attention.

Winfrey's ten-thousand-dollar donation couldn't buy votes, but it gave Tubbs the backing to run a real campaign and drew unprecedented media attention. In November of 2012, the *Stockton Record* reported that Michael Tubbs had won the election by 60 percent.

Where the Riches Come From

Oprah has made most of her fortune from the success of her television show, but what keeps people coming back is her rich inner self and readiness to share. During an interview at Stanford, a business student asked Winfrey how she is able to give so much—not just of her money, but also of her time and attention. Winfrey replied that she is able to give to others because she gives to herself:

> *You've got to decide, how [you are] going to use your money, your talent, your time in such a way that it's going to serve you first—because if it doesn't allow you to be filled up then you'll get depleted and you can't keep doing it.*

The *New York Times* said of Winfrey's philanthropy: "The self-made billionaire appears to spend as freely and gleefully on friends, strangers and the needy as herself." Freely giving to both oneself and to others might seem like opposing goals, but Winfrey believes that knowing who you are—and being proud of who you are—is essential to doing good in the world.

When her "daughters" from the Academy in South Africa begin to ask what majors they should pursue, Winfrey tries to redirect them. It might seem like strange advice from one of the most successful career women on earth, but she tells them: "A career is not a life. What you want to do should emerge from who you want to be. *Who do you want to be?* That, to me, is the essential question."

Winfrey asks her viewers as well as herself: "Who are you when success brings you prosperity, when you get to see and do things that some people can only dream of? Can you remain humble, clear, and mindful of others?"

CHAPTER SIX

What's in Store

The media mogul's talent, generosity, and successes are traits that have been acknowledged in the media industry as well as by cultural and charitable organizations. She has received some of the most prestigious awards available in the United States for her work in many fields. From accolades for her work on *The Oprah Winfrey Show* to recognition for her humanitarian work in the United States and abroad, it seems there isn't an award out there that Oprah Winfrey hasn't won or been nominated for.

Oprah Winfrey continues to win awards for her acting performances, philanthropic contributions, and television programming.

Praise in All Shapes and Sizes

Oprah's awards go back to that first Elks Lodge speech contest in 1970, but once her show got started, many more honors followed. Beginning in 1987, *The Oprah Winfrey Show* garnered much praise and attention. The show received forty-seven Daytime Emmy awards before Winfrey removed the show from consideration in 2000. It continued to be the top-rated talk show in the country, and Winfrey believed it was time to give someone else a shot at those prestigious awards.

The National Association for the Advancement of Colored People (NAACP) has made a tradition of honoring Winfrey for her many contributions to advancing people of color in mainstream media. Her NAACP awards range from Outstanding Talk Show in 1989 to Entertainer of the Year in 1991, and an induction to their Hall of Fame in 2005. Winfrey received four NAACP nominations in 2015 alone for the programming on OWN.

Winfrey also won a Peabody Award in 1995. The award "[spotlights] instances of how electronic media can teach, expand our horizons, defend the public interest, or encourage empathy with others." The Peabody Award recognizes excellence in broadcasting much in the way the Pulitzer Prize recognizes great journalism and literature. During the Peabody Award ceremony, Winfrey's contributions were cited thus:

> *As chair of Harpo Entertainment Group, [Oprah Winfrey] joins the elite company of Lucille Ball and Mary Pickford as the only women in television and film to own their own studios. Her commitment to empowering women and to improving the lives of children is reflected in her charitable and philanthropic work.*

In 1998, Oprah won the S. Roger Horchow Award for Greatest Public Service by a Private Citizen from the Jefferson Awards Foundation. The foundation focuses on empowering individuals to be good citizens and inspiring others to take action—an objective almost no one fills quite as completely as Winfrey. As evidenced by her dedication to helping people create positive change in their communities, Winfrey embodies the Jefferson Award Foundation's mission perfectly.

In addition to the many organizations and foundations that have honored Winfrey and her work, her viewers also stand behind her. From 1988 to 2008, she was nominated for or won a People's Choice Award eight times. The People's Choice Awards recognize contributions to popular culture and are voted on by the general public.

In 2010, Winfrey experienced a great achievement in the form of a Kennedy Center Honor. She was recognized for her lifetime contribution to American arts and culture. Winfrey didn't see that as a signal to stop doing her life's work. In many ways, she was just getting started.

The Presidential Medal of Freedom

After receiving endless recognition for her contributions to television and charity, along with the admiration of millions of viewers, there was still one award that even Oprah Winfrey never dreamed of receiving.

In what Winfrey describes as the "greatest honor in [her] life," President Barack Obama awarded her the Presidential Medal of Freedom in 2013. The Presidential Medal of Freedom is considered the highest civilian honor in the country. The medal was established by former president John F. Kennedy and is awarded to individuals who have made important contributions to to the United States, especially in regard to US national interests, cultural achievements, and the promotion of world peace. President Obama began his speech by joking that he was used to people telling him that he should change his name, just as Oprah was told, early in her career, that she should change her name to Susie. He continued: "People can relate to Susie, that's what they said. It turned out, surprisingly, that people could relate to Oprah just fine." But then President Obama's speech turned more serious. He said:

In more than 4,500 episodes of her show, her message was always, "You can." "You can do and you can be and you can grow and it can be better." And she was living proof, rising from a childhood of poverty and abuse to the pinnacle of the entertainment universe ... Oprah's greatest strength has always been her ability to help us discover the best in ourselves. Michelle and I count ourselves among her many devoted fans and friends. As one of those fans wrote, "I didn't know I had a light in me until Oprah told me it was there." What a great gift.

Later in the ceremony, Winfrey's major contributions were listed as President Obama placed the medal around her neck:

Oprah G. Winfrey is a global media icon. When she launched The Oprah Winfrey Show in 1986, there were few women and even fewer women of color with a national platform to discuss the issues and events facing our times. But over the twenty-five years that followed, Oprah Winfrey's innate gift for tapping into our most fervent hopes and deepest fears drew millions of viewers across every background, making her show the highest-rated talk show in television history. Off screen, Oprah Winfrey has used her influence to support underserved communities and lift up the lives of young people, especially young women, around the world. In her story we are reminded that no dream can be deferred when we refuse to let life's obstacles keep us down.

More Work to be Done

Now that Oprah Winfrey owns not just a show but an entire television channel, are there any challenges left for her to take on?

Winfrey's work continues in many ways. Though she closed The Angel Network when she ended her show, Winfrey continues to give financially to many charities and to help sustain the Oprah Winfrey Leadership Academy for Girls in South Africa. Winfrey doesn't just lavish the girls with an amazing school; she has put mentoring programs in place and flown them to America to attend the play *The Color Purple* on Broadway.

True to Winfrey's intention, her charity is about deep personal connections and lasting change. Even when she was accused of funding the school too frivolously, Winfrey defends the Academy. She is adamant that by fully supporting the few girls who have the privilege of going through the program, more lives will be changed. Rather than getting a minimal education, these girls will be better prepared to make long-lasting changes when they become leaders themselves.

An old saying states: "Give a man a fish, feed him for a day; teach a man to fish, feed him for a lifetime." Just as in this expression, Winfrey's charitable work is a legacy. Her gifts can be passed down through generations all around the world. Just like her approach to hosting her show, Winfrey uses meaningful connections to spread change further than she would be able to do alone.

A Broader Horizon

As Winfrey told her viewers and the girls in her South African academy, it's not your career that matters but your life's mission. Oprah Winfrey's mission is the never-ending pursuit of human understanding and enlightenment, so her work is never done.

Over the course of her long career, the needs of Winfrey's audience have grown as much as the audience itself. Hosting the evening news as a young college student was a big deal. Nashville was growing rapidly at that time, and being on the news gave her a lot more visibility than reciting poems at church. Yet her program only reached the local population, about 600,000 people in 1970. When she made the move to Baltimore, her audience nearly doubled, to a million viewers. Winfrey's first show in Chicago, *AM Chicago*, was available to three times as many people—roughly three million. When the show was renamed and syndicated, Winfrey was viewed in fourteen million homes across the country. Now that her many shows are available on television as well as online, people can tune into Oprah Winfrey twenty-four hours a day across the globe. Where there was once only one *Oprah Winfrey Show*, there are now many shows with Winfrey's signature approach.

Building a Network

It comes as little surprise that when Winfrey builds a television network it's not just about connecting the

Ways to Give

Though Winfrey has closed the doors on her Angel Network, she regularly promotes charities and opportunities to give through the OWN network.

OWN promotes giving at all levels in many different ways. In one article on Oprah.com about how children can give to charity, author Jean Chatzky writes, "Charitable involvement has been shown to help raise self-esteem, develop social skills, foster an introduction to the greater world, and encourage kids to appreciate their own lifestyle." To get involved, she suggests learning how to give in ways that don't require a lot of money, like sending a card to a friend or visiting a lonely family member.

Another suggestion, good for children and adults alike, is to identify clothes and toys that are no longer being used. Some organizations will refurbish old computers and laptops and send them to schools that don't have the budget for new technology.

Emily Torgrimson, a college student who started a charity after Hurricane Katrina, was featured on Oprah.com. Because she didn't have much money to donate, Torgrimson cooked a huge meal and asked all her friends to pitch in a few dollars. Her expectations were blown away when over one hundred people showed up. Since then, she's started an organization called Eat for Equity, which gives the proceeds from dinner parties to charity. Since it was started in 2011, Eat for Equity has raised over $160,000.

Winfrey has even found a way to make people buying things for themselves benefit others. Her Leadership Academy Foundation receives support every time someone buys an Oprah chai tea drink at Starbucks.

shows with viewers. OWN programming is consistently founded on Winfrey's guiding principles of learning and inclusivity. Though Winfrey told CBS that she couldn't be the entire network, her belief system is the foundation of OWN—and she makes many appearances on it.

One of the shows that Winfrey hosts is *SuperSoul Sunday*. She says the show's intention is to "open the hearts and minds of people, and if you can, drop little pieces of light into their lives so they see themselves differently and see their world differently." Continuing her long tradition of interviewing celebrities, she brings the world's leading thinkers and activists on the show to ask life's big questions.

Winfrey has used the show to talk to leaders, like former president Jimmy Carter, and famous authors, like Elizabeth Gilbert, who wrote *Eat, Pray, Love*. Some of her guests have lived through terrifying wars and emerged to help others, like Zainab Salbi. No matter who is featured on the show, there is always a focus on self-discovery and learning to be one's best self.

Back to Her News Anchor Roots

Winfrey also hosts a series called *Where are They Now?* In this show, she follows up on some of the biggest news stories and pop culture icons of the last thirty years, as well as former guests of *The Oprah Winfrey Show*. Though Winfrey herself doesn't host *Oprah's Master Class*, her focus on learning and growing is the show's obvious intention. In this program, celebrities "share their successes, their failures, their triumphs, disappointments, and heartbreaks."

Other shows on the network focus on similar themes ranging from therapeutic guidance to home decorating. In *Iyanla: Fix My Life*, talk show host Iyanla Vanzant follows in Winfrey's footsteps. Talking to everyone from celebrity athletes to ordinary people with big problems, Iyanla uses what she's learned through her own struggles to help others find solutions to their biggest obstacles. *Home Made Simple* is a home improvement show in which couples struggling to remodel their homes are given practical advice to help them finish their projects. Even the handful of reality shows on the network focus on families and celebrities working to overcome life's many challenges so they can achieve their dreams.

While many of the shows reflect Winfrey's intention to help people live better lives, she has also welcomed the assistance of friend and famed director, Tyler Perry. Perry's first contribution to the network, *The Haves and the Have Nots*, helped the channel get on track financially by bringing in a huge viewing audience. The OWN network has since added three more fictional shows directed by Tyler Perry to its roster.

His dramatic tales of romance and scandal may seem like a leap from Winfrey's calming mantra of living your best life, but Perry is also known for adding moral lessons to his scripts. His lessons frequently center on family and honesty. Through lies and dramatic betrayal, Perry's characters learn the value of being good to each other

Tyler Perry's programming for the OWN Network has been among its most successful.

and themselves the hard way. The theatrical scripts are a different approach to answer the same questions Winfrey has spent her career asking. It is also an approach that draws millions of viewers and keeps them coming back for more.

A Leading Lady

In the wake of Winfrey's success in the world of nonfiction—reporting and interviewing—the media mogul seems intent on exploring the possibilities of fiction. She not only provides a network for Perry's hit shows but is taking on more scripts of her own. A long way from going into an interview without any questions prepared, Winfrey says she's excited about the new direction. After all, she left her hugely successful show to take on a new challenge precisely like this. "I love telling the real stories of peoples' lives, and now we get to create them, make them up, and I get to be part of them," the star says of her choice to move the network toward more serial shows.

Though it was early in her career, Winfrey often credits acting in *The Color Purple* as one of the most rewarding experiences of her professional life. In 1998, Winfrey acted in the film *Beloved*, based on a book by Toni Morrison. When it came out, it faced steep competition at the box office and was seen as a failure. Winfrey cites that as the only time she's been depressed, joking that she only knew it was depression because she'd interviewed so many people about it on her show. In 2013, she reflected on what that experience taught her while preparing for the release of her first film role since *Beloved*. This time, she had grown to appreciate that she had helped make a good movie, even if it wasn't as popular as she'd hoped it would be. "What *Beloved* did for me is it freed me, so I can sit in this space now, fifteen years later, and have absolutely no attachment to how people receive [*The Butler*]," Winfrey reflected.

Of course, with Winfrey's Midas touch, there was little to worry about. After receiving praise for her performance in *The Butler*, Winfrey has been considering more acting roles, including Broadway plays. In 2015, she went to New York to consider a role in *'Night, Mother*, a play about a complex mother-daughter relationship and suicide. After reading the script, Winfrey decided not to take the part because it was too depressing. Winfrey says that acting well requires a lot of dedication, as well

On the heels of her successful performance in *The Butler*, Winfrey seeks new acting opportunities, including some on Broadway.

as giving yourself over to the subject of the play. "I just didn't want to be in the space of suicide every night for six months," she said. She plans to keep looking at other plays, though, as long as they have a happier ending.

Nowhere But Up

From rags to riches, Oprah Winfrey is the embodiment of the American dream. Even when faced with adversity, she's met her challenges head-on.

Since the 1980s, Winfrey has been reshaping the way American television is made. Winfrey has also changed the way people all over the world think of themselves and treat one another. It's hard to predict what projects she will take on next, but with Oprah Winfrey's golden touch, a happy ending is all but guaranteed.

Timeline

1988

Buys her own production studio, Harpo Productions

1974

Winfrey gets her first job in television in Nashville, Tennessee

Oprah Winfrey is born in Kosciusko, Mississippi on January 29

1954

The Oprah Winfrey Show's first episode is aired nationally

1986

Moves to Baltimore, Maryland, to be on the nightly news

1976

2007

The Oprah Winfrey Leadership Academy for Girls opens in South Africa

1996

The Oprah Book Club, the largest book club in the world, gets its start

2011

Oprah buys the Oprah Winfrey Network (OWN) with Discovery

The first issue of *O, The Oprah Magazine* is released

2000

After twenty-five years as the top-rated daytime television show, *The Oprah Winfrey Show* ends

2011

SOURCE NOTES

Chapter 1

Page 4: "Oprah On How Faith Helped Her Through Difficult Moments in Her Childhood," *Belief*, October 6, 2015, www.youtu.be/JqLE6OXptwM.

Page 6: "Oprah's Dad-Vernon Winfrey, Nashville," June 17, 2011, www.youtube.com/watch?v=U4JCGM-hWl7I.

Page 6: Henley, William Ernest, "Invictus," Poetry Foundation, www.poetryfoundation.org/poem/182194.

Page 7: "Oprah's Teen Pregnancy Leads to a Second Chance," *Oprah's Lifeclass*, October 20, 2011, www.youtu.be/KrnxCahBJTM.

Page 8: *Ibid.*

Page 9: "An ABC News Barbara Walters Special: Oprah," *ABC*: Barbara Walters Interview, December 2010, www.youtube.com/watch?v=A_MsmbERGmg&feature=youtu.be.

Page 9: Winfrey, Oprah, "Oprah Talks to Graduates about Feelings, Failure, and Finding Happiness," Stanford University, June 15, 2008, news.stanford.edu/news/2008/june18/como-061808.html.

Chapter 2

Page 10: "Celebrities' First Jobs," Oprah.com, November 3, 2009, www.oprah.com/entertainment/Oprahs-Live-Newscast-and-Celebrities-First-Jobs.

Page 10: *Ibid.*

Page 10: *Ibid.*

Page 11: Richman, Alan, "TV's Queen of Talk," *People Magazine*, January 12, 1987. Accessed November 10, 2015. www.people.com/people/archive/article/0,,20095399,00.html.

Page 11: "Celebrities' First Jobs."

Page 11: Kelley, Kitty. *Oprah: A Biography.* (New York: Three Rivers Press, 2010), E-reader.

Page 11: *Ibid.*

Page 11: *Ibid.*

Page 11: Zurawik, David, "Oprah – Built in Baltimore," *Baltimore Sun*, May 18, 2011, articles.baltimoresun.com/2011-05-18/entertainment/bs-sm-oprahs-baltimore-20110522_1_oprah-winfrey-show-baltimore-history-wjz.

Page 12: *Ibid.*

Page 12: *Ibid.*

Page 13: Kelly, *Oprah: A Biography*.

Page 14: "Declaration of Sentiments," Woman's Rights Convention at Seneca Falls, July 1848, Rutgers University, ecssba.rutgers.edu/docs/seneca.html.

Page 14: "Makers Profile: Oprah Winfrey," Makers.com, http://www.makers.com/oprah-winfrey.

Page 15: Richman, "TV's Queen of Talk."

Chapter 3

"Oprah's Disastrous First Show in Chicago," Oprah.com, November 14, 2005, www.oprah.com/oprahshow/ Oprahs-Disastrous-First-Show-in-Chicago-Video.

Page 17: "Memorable Moments," Oprah.com, January 1, 2006. www.oprah.com/oprahshow/Memorable-Moments.

Page 18: Eum, Jennifer, "How Oprah Went from Talk Show Host to First African-American Billionaire," Forbes, September 29, 2014. Accessed November 28, 2015, www.forbes.com/sites/jennifereum/2014/09/29/how-oprah-went-from-talkshow-host-to-first-african-american-woman-billionaire.

Page 18: "Makers Profile: Oprah Winfrey."

Page 18: "The Michael Jackson Interview: Oprah Reflects," Oprah.com, September, 16, 2009.

Page 20: "Oprah Winfrey on Career, Life and Leadership," Stanford Graduate School of Business, April 28, 2014, www.youtube.com/watch?v=6DlrqeWrczs.

Page 21: *Ibid*.

Page 21: Robins, J. Max, "Oprah's OWN Makeover: From Failure to Success," December 12, 2013, www.forbes.com/sites/maxrobins/2013/12/12/oprahs-own-makeover-from-failure-to-success.

Page 21: Rose, Lacy, "Oprah Winfrey on Forgoing Motherhood, Being 'Counted Out' and the Meeting that Turned OWN Around," December 11, 2013, www.hollywoodreporter.com/news/oprah-winfrey-forgoing-motherhood-being-664550.

Page 22: King, Gayle and Charlie Rose, "Oprah Winfrey on OWN Mistakes and Never Quitting," CBS This Morning, April 22, 2012, www.cbsnews.com/news/oprah-winfrey-on-own-mistakes-and-never-quitting.

Chapter 4

Page 23: Tannen, Deborah, "Oprah Winfrey: The TV Host," Time Magazine, June 8, 1988. content.time.com/time/magazine/article/0,9171,988512,00.html.

Page 24: "What Oprah Knows for Sure about Growing Up," *O: The Oprah Magazine*, May 2001, www.oprah.com/spirit/Oprahs-Lessons-About-Growing-Up.

Chapter 5

Page 30: "Oprah Winfrey on Career, Life and Leadership."

Page 30: Curnow, Robyn and Teo Kermeliotis, "Oprah a 'Proud Momma' As First Academy Students Graduate," CNN, January 25, 2012. Accessed November 20, 2015, www.cnn.com/2012/01/25/business/oprah-winfrey-leadership-academy.

Page 30: *Ibid.*

Page 30: *Ibid.*

Page 31: *Ibid.*

Page 31: Van Fleet, Justin W., "Africa's Education Crisis: In School But Not Learning," Brookings Institute, September 17, 2012, www.brookings.edu/blogs/up-front/posts/2012/09/17-africa-education-crisis-van-fleet.

Page 31: *Ibid.*

Page 34: "Mayor Cory Booker's Political Future," Oprah's Next Chapter, May 29, 2012. www.youtube.com/watch?v=hEnn_zEI2a0.

Page 34: Smith, Scott, "Oprah Gives $10k to Stockton Candidate," Recordnet.com, May 19, 2012. Accessed November 29, 2015, www.recordnet.com/apps/pbcs.dll/article?AID=/20120519/A_NEWS/205190320.

Page 35: "Oprah Winfrey on Career, Life and Leadership."

Page 35: Stanley, Alessandra, "Oh, Oprah, 20 Years of Talk, Causes and Self-Improvement," *New York Times,* November 15, 2005, www.nytimes.com/2005/11/15/arts/television/oh-oprah-20-years-of-talk-causes-and-selfimprovement.html.

Page 35: "What Oprah Knows for Sure About Asking the Right Questions," Oprah.com, March 18, 2014, www.oprah.com/spirit/What-Oprah-Knows-for-Sure-About-Asking-The-Right-Questions.

Page 35: *Ibid.*

Chapter 6

Page 36: "Message from the Director," The Peabody Awards, www.peabodyawards.com/about.

Page 36: "Personal Award: Oprah Winfrey," 1995, www.peabodyawards.com/award-profile/personal-award-oprah-winfrey.

Page 37: "Remarks By the President at Presidential Medal of Freedom Ceremony." November 20, 2013, www.whitehouse.gov/the-press-office/2013/11/20/remarks-president-presidential-medal-freedom-ceremony.

Page 38: *Ibid.*

Page 39: Chatzky, Jean, "Six Steps to Raising Money-Savvy Kids," January 27, 20011, www.oprah.com/money/How-to-Teach-Your-Kids-About-Money-Jean-Chatzky

Page 40: "Oprah Sits Down with humanitarian Zainab Salbi," *Super Soul Sunday*, November 23, 2015, www.youtube.com/watch?v=jsfub6vwcMM.

Page 40: "Oprah's Master Class," www.oprah.com/app/master-class.html.

Page 41: Rose, "Oprah Winfrey on Forgoing Motherhood, Being 'Counted Out' and the Meeting that Turned OWN Around."

Page 41: Suskind, Alex, "Oprah Winfrey on 'Lee Daniels' The Butler,' Returning to the Big Screen, and the Commercial Failure of 'Beloved'," August 8, 2013, mfblog.aol.ca/2013/08/08/oprah-winfrey-lee-daniels-the-butler-interview.

Page 41: Rose, "Oprah Winfrey on Forgoing Motherhood, Being 'Counted Out' and the Meeting that Turned OWN Around."

GLOSSARY

audition A trial given to a performer when being considered for a job or performance.

civil rights A class of rights that protect individuals, often minorities, from governmental discrimination.

confrontational television A type of television programming popular in the 1990s where hosts would encourage violent and dramatic arguments between guests.

discrimination The practice of treating someone better or worse than others based on factors such as race, class, or gender.

Emmy Award A national award which recognizes excellence in television.

empathy The ability to share and understand the feelings of others.

endorsement Giving public support or approval for a person or product.

feminism The belief that women are equal to men and should be treated as equals socially, politically, and economically.

intention An objective, especially one that reaches beyond the work necessary to achieve the goal itself.

media mogul A businessperson who controls a large portion of media outlets through ownership and/or position.

network A channel of shows available on television that is owned by one or multiple parent companies.

newsreader Someone on a news program who reads live news from cue cards or a teleprompter.

orator A skilled public speaker.

philanthropist Someone who promotes the wellbeing of others, usually through large monetary donations.

public service announcement (PSA) Messages produced by the media free of charge, which are typically aimed at improving public health or education.

segregation The enforced separation of different groups, historically based on race.

social issues A problem or conflict that influences and is opposed by many individuals in a society.

syndication Licensing the right for individual stations to broadcast an independently-produced program.

FURTHER INFORMATION

Books

Editors of O, *The Oprah Magazine*. O's Little Book of Happiness. New York, NY: Flatiron Books, 2015.

Hoose, Phillip. *Claudette Colvin: Twice Toward Justice.* New York, NY: Square Fish, 2010.

Lowe, Janet. *Oprah Winfrey Speaks: Insights from the World's Most Influential Voice.* New York, NY: John Wiley & Sons, 1998.

Walker, Alice. *The Color Purple.* New York, NY: Pocket Books, 1982.

Winfrey, Oprah. *What I Know for Sure. London, UK: Macmillan Books, 2014.*

Websites

The Leader in Me
www.theleaderinme.org
Students can learn leadership tips from this educational site.

Money As You Grow
www.moneyasyougrow.org
Endorsed by the American Library Foundation, this site is a resource to help kids make smart financial choices.

Oprah.com
Oprah.com
Oprah.com shares information about Oprah Winfrey and the OWN network, including videos from famous interviews and an official biography of the star.

Oprah Winfrey Leadership Academy for Girls
www.owla.co.za
The Oprah Winfrey Leadership Academy for Girls website tells the story of the school's founding and its state-of-the-art facilities. The site also gives information about supporting the school through donations.

Public Broadcast Station
www.pbs.org
The Public Broadcasting Service (PBS) provides information on current events as well as special reports on topics of public interest.

US History

www.ushistory.org

USHistory.org offers information on a wide range of events in the history of the United States of America. Learn more about the early foundations of feminism in the website's archives.

Video

The Color Purple

www.amazon.com/Color-Purple-Whoopi-Goldberg/dp/
   B00LFE3YM

The Color Purple, a film based on the novel by Alice Walker, was Winfrey's debut as an actress. Her performance in the film earned nominations for some of the entertainment industry's most prestigious awards.

BIBLIOGRAPHY

"An ABC News Barbara Walters Special: Oprah." December 2010. Barbara Walters Interview, 11:53. Posted December 2010. www.youtube.com/watch?v=A_MsmbERGmg&feature=youtu.be.

Curnow, Robyn and Teo Kermeliotis. "Oprah a 'Proud Momma' As First Academy Students Graduate." CNN.com, January 25, 2012. Accessed November 20, 2015. www.cnn.com/2012/01/25/business/oprah-winfrey-leadership-academy.

Eum, Jennifer. "How Oprah Went from Talk Show Host to First African-American Billionaire." Forbes, September 29, 2014. www.forbes.com/sites/jennifereum/2014/09/29/how-oprah-went-from-talk-show-host-to-first-african-american-woman-billionaire.

Haggerty, Ryan. "Giving to Chicago and Beyond." Chicago Tribune. May 20, 2011. articles.chicagotribune.com/2011-05-20/entertainment/ct-ae-0522-oprah-causes-metro-20110520_1_philanthropy-harpo-janice-peck

Kelley, Kitty. *Oprah: A Biography*. New York, NY: Three Rivers Press, 2010.

King, Gayle and Charlie Rose. "Oprah Winfrey on OWN Mistakes and Never Quitting." CBS This Morning.

Video, 9:23. April 22, 2012. www.cbsnews.com/news/
oprah-winfrey-on-own-mistakes-and-never-quitting.

Krohn, Katherine E. *Oprah Winfrey: Global Media Leader.*
Minneapolis, MN: Lerner Pub Group, 2008.

Levin, Gary. "Oprah Isn't Quite Holding Her OWN." USA
Today. March 21, 2012. usatoday30.usatoday.com/life/
television/news/story/2012-03-20/own-oprah-cut-jobs.

NPR Staff. "Oprah Hopes Her Midas Touch Gilds Her
OWN Series, 'Belief'." *Morning Edition.* October 20,
2015. www.npr.org/2015/10/20/450102309/oprah-
hopes-her-midas-touch-gilds-her-own-series-belief.

"Oprah's Teen Pregnancy Leads to a Second Chance."
Filmed October 2011. *Oprah's Lifeclass,*
3:43. youtu.be/KrnxCahBJTM.

"Oprah On How Faith Helped Her Through Difficult
Moments in Her Childhood." Filmed 2015. youtu.be/
JqLE6OXptwM.

Pech, Janice. "The Secret of Her Success: Oprah Winfrey
and the Seduction of Self-Transformation." *Journal of
Communication Inquiry* (2010): Vol. 34 no. 1. jci.sage-
pub.com/content/34/1/7.abstract.

Richman, Alan. "TV's Queen of Talk." *People Magazine,*
January 12, 1987. www.people.com/people/archive/arti-
cle/0,,20095399,00.html.

Slack, Megan. "President Obama Honors Presidential Medal of Freedom Recipients." November 20, 2013. www.whitehouse.gov/blog/2013/11/20/president-obama-honors-presidential-medal-freedom-recipients.

Smith, Scott. "Oprah Gives $10k to Stockton Candidate." May 19, 2012. www.recordnet.com/apps/pbcs.dll/article?AID=/20120519/A_NEWS/205190320.

Trombino, Dominic and Britni Day. "*Oprah: From Chicago to the World.*" www.nbcchicago.com/news/local/Oprahs-Chicago-History-122362959.html.

Van Fleet, Justin W. "Africa's Education Crisis: In School But Not Learning." www.brookings.edu/blogs/up-front/posts/2012/09/17-africa-education-crisis-van-fleet.

Winfrey, Oprah. "Oprah Talks to Graduates about Feelings, Failure, and Finding Happiness." news.stanford.edu/news/2008/june18/como-061808.html.

Zimmerman, Kim Ann. ""Hurricane Katrina: Facts, Damage & Aftermath." www.livescience.com/22522-hurricane-katrina-facts.html.

INDEX

Page numbers in **boldface** are illustrations. Entries in **boldface** are glossary terms.

ABOUT THE AUTHOR

Tatiana Ryckman is a writer, editor, and teacher from Cleveland, Ohio. She received a Master's degree in Creative Writing from Vermont College of Fine Arts and currently resides in Austin, Texas. Her publications include a collection of short stories, *Twenty-Something*, as well as articles and poems in a variety of literary journals. When she is not writing, she enjoys reading and bicycling with friends.